SPIRIT WRITER

EXPLORING THE ENIGMA OF THE SPIRIT WORLD

WENDY SHEFFIELD

Spiritwriterspeaks

Previous publications include:

Spirit Writer: A Journey of Spiritual Awakening and Self-Discovery
(Books 1-4)

Series of spiritual books published in 2024
The Devil Within: Evil In This World Today
Spirit Writer: This Journey Called Life
Spirit Writer: The Spirit Guide Connection
Spirit Writer: The Enigma of the Spirit World

Cover image copyright to leonid_tit purchased from istock.com
Designed by Author: Wendy Sheffield

This book is published by SPIRITWRITERSPEAKS

A CIP record for this book is available from the British Library.

I would like to extend my sincerest dedication to all those who are in pursuit of knowledge, both in this world and the next.

I hope my Spiritual Books aid you in your journey.

May you find the courage within yourselves to search relentlessly for what you seek.

Wendy

Life In The Spirit World

Life in the Spirit World is a realm where souls find liberation, love transcends boundaries, and eternal connection becomes our ultimate reality.

In the Spirit World, life is free from the constraints of time and space, where souls dance to the rhythm of eternal harmony.

The Spirit World reminds us that our journey of life doesn't end with death, but rather transcends into a realm of boundless possibilities and eternal growth.

* * *

Life is when the Spirit World reminds us that our existence extends beyond this earthly plan, awakening our souls to the infinite possibilities that await us on the other side.

The essence of life in the Spirit World lies not in its physical manifestation, but in the boundless realm of consciousness and spiritual growth.

Contents

Spirit's Wish For Mankind

The conception of the author's second book, Pure Spirit, was deeply influenced by her understanding that a profound aspiration of the Spiritual Universe is for humankind to attain a unified consciousness, transcending linguistic and cultural differences. Thus, in light of this perspective, this literary endeavour undertakes an exploration into the tenets of various principal religions. The intention is to foster mutual comprehension among diverse cultures and advance toward a singular harmonious voice - tantamount to what Spirit envisages.

Let us collectively reflect upon this significant excerpt...

Many people have many different thoughts.

*Many people only listen to their own thoughts;
understanding them isn't always easy.*

*When there's understanding, there's happiness and
no sadness.*

*We should realise we're not alone.
Spirit sends love to us and words that are needed.
When we're all aware, people will understand.*

*The knowledge comes down to everyone who's
ready to receive it.*

*Some people may question Spirit intelligence, but
the knowledge only comes to those that are ready
for it.*

*Ask, and the true meaning of love will come to us,
and then everyone will be together as one.*

*We'll be one voice, with no separation of language.
We'll understand each other.*

*When people work together and stand together,
they won't stand apart, and everyone will share the
love.*

Spirit's Wish For Mankind

Stop and listen. Stop and share!

Channelled by Wendy Sheffield, first published in Pure Spirit, the second book on the Author's life.

Introduction

Spirit World: Exploring the Enigma of The Spirit World

By Wendy Sheffield

The Spirit World has long been a subject of fascination and speculation among believers and skeptics alike.

In *"Exploring the Enigma Of The Spirit World"*, author Sheffield takes readers on a profound journey through the realms beyond our physical existence in the hope that they will open their hearts and minds in order to learn what Spirit wants them to learn.

Drawing from extensive research and personal experiences, Sheffield delves into the mysteries of the Spirit World, providing a comprehensive analysis of its nature, purpose, and impact on our lives.

Whether you are a curious skeptic or a firm believer, this book offers valuable insights and thought-provoking considerations on the enigma of life beyond the tangible realm.

In the realm of the Spirit World, time holds no significance as beings exist in a perpetual present. While this concept may be difficult for us mortal beings to grasp, we can gain deeper insights into life in the Spirit World through the words of my Spirit guide.

"In this ethereal realm, thoughts and intentions instantly manifest into reality. Every aspect of what you perceive is a reflection of the energy you emit.

The Spirit realm serves as a nurturing space for personal growth, learning, and unconditional love.

Within this harmonious existence, all beings support one another's Spiritual evolution.

It is within our minds that the paradise known as the Spirit World takes shape.

Even here in the physical realm, you possess the

power to spread love and kindness, ultimately transforming your surroundings.

By demonstrating understanding and positivity, each individual has the capacity to make a significant impact wherever they go.

While you may not currently reside in the Spirit World at this moment in time, you have the ability to create a
fragment of it right here and now.

Each of us holds ultimate control over our own destiny, that is the reason that it is important to take responsibility for your own actions in the here and now so that you will be ready when your time is right to join our brothers and sisters in the hereafter.

Channelled by Wendy Sheffield

Part 1

Defining the Spirit World: What is it?

Before diving into the depths of the Spirit World, it is essential to establish a clear understanding of what exactly it encompasses.

The Spirit World can be described as a realm or dimension that exists beyond the limitations of our physical reality. It is a realm inhabited by spirits, entities, and energies that are separate from our material existence.

While the concept of the Spirit World is often associated with religious beliefs, it is not limited to any particular faith or belief system. In fact, various cultures and religions around the world acknowledge existence of the Spirit World, although they may have different interpretations and understandings of it.

In this comprehensive analysis, Sheffield aims to present a holistic view of the Spirit World that goes beyond religious dogma. By drawing from a range of sources, including ancient texts, modern literature, and personal accounts, Wendy provides a nuanced understanding of this enigmatic realm.

Stay tuned to consider the Spirit World through the eyes of various religious sects.

As the author is a spiritualist, she has also included a chapter on the *Spirit World Through The Eyes Of a Spiritualist (Chapter 2)*.

The author truly believes that the spiritualist religion will be the religion of the New Age when we all understand each other....

Chapter 1

The Spirit World through the eyes of a Christian

From the perspective of a Christian, the Spirit World is a topic of much intrigue and debate. It is believed that within this realm exists the supernatural, a realm where angels and demons reside, where spiritual battles are fought, and where the eternal destiny of souls is determined.

In Christianity, the Spirit World is seen as a powerful force that has the ability to influence our lives in both positive and negative ways. It is believed that God created the Spirit World and that it is part of His divine plan. The Bible tells us that there are both good and evil spirits, with God being the ultimate authority over all.

While the Spirit World is not visible to the naked eye, Christians believe that it can be discerned

3

through prayer, scripture, and the guidance of the Holy Spirit. Christians also believe that angels, which are seen as heavenly beings, are sent by God to protect and guide His people. They are seen as messengers of God, delivering His divine will to those on earth.

On the other hand, Christians also believe in the existence of demonic forces that seek to deceive and tempt humans away from God. These evil spirits are believed to be fallen angels who rebelled against God and are now enemies of humanity. Christians are encouraged to resist these evil forces and to rely on the power of God to overcome them.

While the Spirit World may seem mysterious and complex, Christians believe that through their faith in Jesus Christ, they can have a personal relationship with God and access the power of the Holy Spirit. This relationship allows them to navigate the challenges of life and find comfort and guidance in the midst of spiritual battles.

In conclusion, the Spirit World from the eyes of a Christian is a realm of supernatural forces that has a profound impact on human lives. It is believed to be a realm where angels and demons exist, where spiritual battles are fought, and where the eternal destiny of souls is determined. Through prayer, scripture, and the guidance of the Holy Spirit, Christians seek to understand and navigate this realm, relying on their faith in Jesus Christ to overcome evil and find comfort and guidance in their daily lives.

Chapter 2

The Spirit World through the eyes of a Spiritualist

The Spirit World is a concept that has intrigued and fascinated humans for centuries. Many people, especially those who consider themselves spiritualists, believe in the existence of an afterlife and the presence of spirits in our world. They believe that the Spirit World is a realm where souls reside after death, and where they continue to exist in some form or another.

A spiritualist's view of the Spirit World encompasses a vast and intriguing realm that exists beyond the physical plane of existence. Spiritualists believe in the existence of spirits or souls who continue to exist after death, and they believe in communication with these spirits. This view is rooted in the belief that there is more to life than what meets the eye, that there is a spiritual dimension that is interconnected with the physical one.

In the Spirit World, spirits are said to be able to communicate with the living through mediums who have the ability to connect with them. Mediums act as a bridge between the physical and spiritual realms, receiving messages and guidance from spirits and relaying them to the living. These communications often bring comfort, reassurance, and healing to those who have lost loved ones.

Spiritualists believe that the Spirit World is not only a place for departed souls, but also a source of wisdom, knowledge, and guidance. Spirits are seen as wise and compassionate beings who can offer insights and guidance to those who seek it. They may provide answers to life's questions, offer advice on important decisions, or simply offer comfort and support.

Furthermore, spiritualists suggest that the Spirit World is not limited to souls who have passed away. They believe that spirits can also include beings from other dimensions and planes of existence, such as angels, ascended masters, and spirit guides. These higher beings are thought to be enlightened and evolved souls who have chosen to help and guide others in their earthly journey.

In conclusion, for Spiritualists, the Spirit World is a realm of existence beyond the physical, where souls continue their journey of growth and evolution. It is a place of wisdom, guidance, and healing, where spirits can communicate with the living through mediums. While the existence of the Spirit World is a matter of personal belief, for those who embrace spiritualism, it offers comfort, reassurance, and a deeper understanding of life and death.

Chapter 3

The Spirit World through the eyes of a Jew

Judaism has a long and rich history, filled with mystical teachings and beliefs about the afterlife. While the Jewish faith primarily focuses on life in this world, there are also various teachings that delve into the realms of the Spirit World.

As a Jew, the concept of the Spirit World holds great significance and plays a vital role in their religious beliefs and practices. The Spirit World, also known as the afterlife, is a realm where the souls of the deceased reside and where they continue their spiritual journey after death.

In Judaism, the belief in the Spirit World is deeply rooted in their ancient scriptures and teachings. The Torah, their Holy Book, contains numerous references to the existence of an afterlife. It is believed that after death, the soul transitions to the world to come, known as *Olam HaBa*. This world is said to be a place of reward and punishment, where the righteous are blessed and the wicked face consequences for their actions in their earthly life.

For Jews, the Spirit World is not just a distant concept, but rather something that they actively engage with on a daily basis. They are encouraged to remember and honour their ancestors, to keep their memories alive and to connect with them spiritually. This is done through prayers, rituals, and observances such as visiting their graves, reciting the Kaddish prayer, and lighting Yahrzeit candles on the anniversary of their passing.

Furthermore, the Spirit World plays a significant role in their understanding of justice and accountability. The belief in an ultimate judgment, where each individual is held accountable for their actions, serves as a powerful moral compass in their lives. It reminds them to live their lives with integrity, compassion, and righteousness, knowing that their actions will ultimately be judged in the Spirit World.

At the same time, the concept of the Spirit World brings comfort and solace in times of grief and loss. The belief that their loved ones continue to exist in another realm, watching over us, provides a sense of connection and hope. It allows them to find meaning in their sorrow and to find strength in the knowledge that death is not the end, but rather a transition to another plane of existence.

In conclusion, as a Jew, the Spirit World holds deep meaning and importance in their faith. It serves as a reminder of their moral responsibilities, a source of comfort in times of loss, and a connection to their ancestors. The belief in the Spirit World is not just a theoretical concept, but rather something that influences their daily lives and guides our actions. It is a testament to the enduring nature of the Jewish faith and its emphasis on the eternal nature of the human soul.

Chapter 4
The Spirit World through the eyes of a Hindu

Hinduism, one of the oldest religions in the world, has a unique and complex view of the Spirit World. The Hindu belief system is deeply rooted in the concept of a multi-dimensional reality, where the physical and spiritual realms intertwine. According to Hindu philosophy, the Spirit World is inhabited by various celestial beings, spirits, and deities.

In Hinduism, the Spirit World is seen as a vast and interconnected web of existence. It is believed that the Spirit World is populated by both benevolent and malevolent entities, each with their own unique roles and responsibilities. These entities can include gods and goddesses, as well as lesser beings such as demigods, nature spirits, and ancestors.

One of the central beliefs in Hinduism is the concept of reincarnation, whereby the soul is believed to pass through various physical bodies in a cyclical process. This belief holds that the Spirit World is the realm where the soul resides in between its physical incarnations. The Spirit World is seen as a place where the soul undergoes rest, reflection, and preparation for its next incarnation.

In Hindu mythology, many gods and goddesses play significant roles in the Spirit World. These deities are often worshipped and revered by Hindus, who believe that they have the power to influence the course of human life. Some of the most popular gods and goddesses include Brahma, Vishnu, Shiva, Lakshmi, and Saraswati. Each of these deities has specific attributes and responsibilities, and Hindus often pray to them for guidance, protection, and blessings.

In addition to gods and goddesses, Hinduism also places great importance on ancestor worship. Hindus believe that the spirits of deceased family members continue to exist in the Spirit World, and they can be honoured and communicated with through rituals and prayers. Ancestor worship is seen as a way to maintain a connection with one's lineage and to seek the guidance and blessings of one's ancestors.

Overall, the Hindu view of the Spirit World is rich and intricate, reflecting the complexities of human existence and the interconnectedness of all beings. It emphasises the importance of spirituality, worship, and devotion in one's daily life and encourages individuals to seek knowledge, enlightenment, and liberation from the cycle of birth and death.

Chapter 5

The Spirit World through the eyes of a Buddhist

Buddhism is a religion that places great emphasis on the concept of impermanence and the interconnectedness of all life forms. When it comes to the Spirit World, Buddhists have a unique perspective that differs from traditional beliefs held by other religions.

In Buddhism, the Spirit World is seen as a realm of existence that is part of the cycle of birth and death. Buddhists believe in the concept of reincarnation, whereby beings are reborn into different existences based on their actions and karma from previous lives. The Spirit World is just one of the many realms in which these rebirths can occur.

Buddhists view the Spirit World as a temporary state, similar to their current human existence. It is believed that beings in the Spirit World are still bound by desire and attachment, which perpetuates the cycle of suffering and rebirth. However, unlike our physical world, the Spirit World is not considered to be a permanent or ultimate reality.

In Buddhism, the ultimate goal is to attain enlightenment and liberation from the cycle of rebirth. This can only be achieved by breaking free from desire, attachment, and ignorance. Therefore, while the Spirit World is acknowledged, it is not a focus of Buddhist teachings. Instead, Buddhists place importance on developing wisdom, compassion, and mindfulness in order to transcend the cycle of suffering and attain liberation.

Furthermore, Buddhists believe that all beings, including those in the Spirit World, have the potential to awaken their true nature and attain liberation. This belief is based on the concept of Buddha-nature, which states that all beings possess the innate capacity for enlightenment.

In Buddhist practice, there are various rituals, meditations, and prayers that can be performed to benefit beings in the Spirit World. These practices are aimed at generating positive karma and helping beings on their path towards liberation.

Overall, Buddhists view the Spirit World as just one part of the vast interconnected web of existence. While it is acknowledged and respected, Buddhists focus on cultivating wisdom and compassion in order to attain liberation from the cycle of suffering. Understanding this perspective is key to gaining insight into the Buddhist approach to the Spirit World.

Chapter 6
Universal Beliefs

The concept of the Spirit World is deeply ingrained in religious beliefs across the globe. While there are significant differences among various religious traditions, when it comes to their understanding of the Spirit World, there are also commonalities that can be found. These commonalities reveal a shared belief in the existence of a spiritual realm that transcends the physical world and plays a significant role in the lives of individuals.

One aspect that most religions agree on is the existence of an afterlife. The afterlife, also known as the Spirit World, is believed to be a realm where the souls of individuals go after death. Religions such as Christianity, Islam, Hinduism, Buddhism, and Judaism all have their own interpretations of the afterlife, but they share the belief in the existence of a spiritual realm where souls continue to exist in some form.

Another common belief regarding the Spirit World is the presence of spiritual beings. These beings are often regarded as supernatural entities or higher powers that have a direct influence on human lives. They are often described as angels, demons, or ancestors, depending on the religious tradition. The belief in the presence of these spiritual beings emphasises the interconnectedness between the physical and spiritual realms.

Furthermore, religions widely concur that human beings possess a soul or a spirit that is distinct from the physical body. This soul is often seen as the essence of a person's identity and consciousness. It is believed to be eternal and capable of transcending physical boundaries. The understanding of the soul may differ across religions, but the foundational belief in a spiritual element within each individual is prevalent.

Moreover, religions agree on the importance of spiritual practices and rituals for connecting with the Spirit World. These practices often involve prayer, meditation, and the observance of religious ceremonies. Through these practices, individuals seek guidance, enlightenment, and a deeper connection with the spiritual realm.

In conclusion, while there may be various interpretations and beliefs surrounding the Spirit World, religions generally agree on its existence, the presence of spiritual beings, the eternal nature of the soul, and the significance of spiritual practices. These shared beliefs reflect the universal human longing for a connection with something greater than the physical world and provide a framework for understanding and engaging with the Spirit World across different religious traditions.

Part 2

The Existence and Role of Spirits in the Spirit World

In this section, we will delve deeper into the existence and role of spirits in the Spirit World.

Spirits play a crucial role in shaping the dynamics of this enigmatic realm. They are believed to be souls of deceased individuals who have transitioned from the physical realm to the spiritual one.

The existence of spirits is widely acknowledged across cultures and belief systems, although their nature and purpose may vary. Some view spirits as benevolent beings guiding and protecting the living, while others consider them as entities that can be both helpful and malevolent.

Understanding the role of spirits in the Spirit World is key to unraveling the mysteries of this dimension.

In the upcoming chapters, we will explore different types of spirits, their characteristics, and how they interact with both the spiritual and physical realms.

Stay tuned to understand the existence and role of spirits in the Spirit World.

Chapter 1
Different Types of Spirits

The Spirit World is a realm believed to exist parallel to our physical world, inhabited by various types of spirits. These spirits are said to possess unique characteristics and powers, and their presence is acknowledged and revered in different cultures and religions around the world.

One of the most commonly known types of spirits in the Spirit World is the ***ancestral spirits***. These spirits are believed to be the souls of deceased family members who continue to watch over and guide their living descendants. In many cultures, ancestor worship is an important part of their belief system, and offering prayers and ceremonies to honour these spirits is a way to ensure their blessings and protection.

Another type of Spirit commonly found in the Spirit World is the **nature spirits** or **elementals**. These spirits are said to reside in natural elements such as trees, rivers, mountains, and even the air we breathe. They are believed to possess a powerful connection to the forces of nature and can influence the world around us. In many indigenous cultures, these spirits are known as **sprites, fairies**, or **nymphs** and are often depicted as benevolent beings who assist in the balance and harmony of the natural world.

In addition, there are also spirits believed to be **celestial beings** or **divine messengers** in the Spirit World. These spirits are often associated with gods, goddesses, or deities and are believed to have a direct connection to the divine. They are revered and worshipped in different religious traditions and are believed to possess immense wisdom and power.

Furthermore, there are spirits known as **guardian spirits** or **spirit guides**. These spirits are believed to be assigned to individuals to protect and guide them throughout their lives. Many people believe that these spirits communicate with us through dreams, visions, and intuition, offering guidance and support during times of need.

Finally, there are spirits that are believed to be **earthbound** or **trapped** in the Spirit World due to unfinished business or unresolved emotions. These spirits are often associated with haunted locations and are said to wander the physical world, seeking closure or redemption. It is believed that through various spiritual practices such as prayers, rituals, and mediumship, these spirits can find peace and move on to the afterlife.

In conclusion, the Spirit World is a diverse realm inhabited by different types of spirits, each with their own unique characteristics and powers. From **ancestral spirits** to **nature spirits, celestial beings** to **guardian spirits**, the presence of these spirits is acknowledged and revered in various cultures and religious traditions around the world. Whether they are worshipped, revered, or sought for guidance, the belief in the Spirit World provides a window into the unseen realms and offers a deeper understanding of the metaphysical aspects of existence.

Chapter 2
How Spirits Interact with Spiritual and Physical Realms

The interaction between spirits and the realms of spirituality and the physical world has been a topic of great fascination and intrigue for centuries. Many individuals believe that there exists a metaphysical plane, separate from our physical reality, where spirits reside and can communicate with the living. These spirits are believed to be the souls of deceased individuals or entities from another Spiritual realm.

In various cultures and religions, the belief in spirits and their interaction with human beings is deeply ingrained. From ancient civilizations to modern societies, countless stories, myths, and religious practices have revolved around the interaction between spirits and the mortal world. These interactions can take different forms, such as apparitions, possession, or communication through mediums or spiritual rituals.

One commonly held belief is that spirits may interact with the physical world through manipulation of energy or objects. Many people claim to have witnessed objects moving on their own, unexplainable sounds, or even the sensation of being touched by an unseen force. These occurrences are often attributed to the presence and influence of spirits.

Additionally, spirits are believed to communicate with the living through mediums or psychics who possess the ability to connect with the spiritual realm. These individuals claim to receive messages from spirits and relay them to those seeking guidance or communication with their deceased loved ones. Spiritual rituals, such as séances or ceremonies, are often performed to facilitate these interactions.

However, the existence and nature of spirits and their interaction with the physical world remains a matter of deep mystery and debate. Skeptics argue that these experiences can be attributed to psychological factors or natural phenomena that are yet to be fully understood. Paranormal investigations and scientific studies have been conducted to explore the validity of these claims, but conclusive evidence is often lacking.

Regardless of the debates, it is undeniable that the belief in spirits and their interaction with the spiritual and physical realms has greatly influenced cultures and societies throughout history. This belief has shaped rituals, customs, and even laws, as people seek to understand and make sense of the supernatural.

In conclusion, the interaction between spirits and the spiritual and physical realms has been a subject of fascination and belief in many cultures. While skeptics may dismiss these experiences as mere superstition, the belief in spirits continues to play a significant role in shaping the beliefs and practices of countless individuals worldwide.

Part 3

Lifecycles in the Spirit World: Birth, Death, and Reincarnation

In this section, we will take a closer look at the lifecycles in the Spirit World, specifically focusing on the processes of birth, death, and reincarnation. These fundamental aspects shed light on the continuous cycle of existence in the Spirit realm.

Birth in the Spirit World is not in the traditional sense we are familiar with. It is more of a transition from one state of being to another. Spirits are believed to enter the Spirit World through various means, such as a spiritual birth or reincarnation, depending on their individual journey and spiritual growth.

Death, on the other hand, is seen as a mere change of state for spirits. It is a liberation from the physical body and a return to the spiritual realm. Unlike in the physical world, death is not the end but a new beginning in the Spirit World.

Reincarnation is a fascinating concept in the Spirit World. It is the belief that Spirits can be reborn into new physical bodies to continue their spiritual growth and experiences. Reincarnation allows spirits to learn and evolve through multiple lifetimes, bringing wisdom and lessons from past incarnations.

Understanding the lifecycles in the Spirit World provides valuable insights into the purpose and journey of spirits. It illustrates the interconnectedness between the physical and spiritual realms, shaping our perception of life, death, and the eternal nature of the Spirit.

Stay tuned to understand the lifecycles in the Spirit World: birth, death, and reincarnation.

Chapter 1
Birth as seen by the Spirit World

The concept of birth in the Spirit World is one that has fascinated human beings for centuries. It is a topic that has been explored in various religions and spiritual beliefs, and holds a special significance for those who hold these beliefs. In this chapter, we will delve deeper into the idea of birth in the Spirit World and its implications.

In many spiritual traditions, birth in the Spirit World is seen as a transition from one realm of existence to another. It is believed that after death, the soul leaves the physical body and enters the Spirit World, where it undergoes a process of rebirth or reincarnation. This process is often seen as a continuation of the soul's spiritual journey, with opportunities for growth, learning, and spiritual evolution.

The idea of birth in the Spirit World brings with it a sense of hope and renewal. It suggests that life does not end with physical death, but rather continues in a different form. This belief can provide comfort and solace to those who have lost loved ones, knowing that their spirits continue to exist and may even be born into a new life.

Moreover, birth in the Spirit World is also associated with the idea of karma and the notion that our actions in this life determine our future experiences. It is believed that the soul is born into a particular situation or circumstance based on its past actions and the lessons it needs to learn. This idea of personal responsibility and accountability adds depth to the concept of birth in the Spirit World, as it suggests that we have the power to shape our own destiny through our thoughts, words, and actions.

Additionally, birth in the Spirit World can be seen as a form of spiritual awakening. It is believed that during this process, the soul gains a deeper understanding of itself and its connection to the divine. This awakening can lead to profound spiritual experiences, enlightenment, and a closer relationship with the divine.

In conclusion, birth in the Spirit World is a multifaceted concept that holds great significance in many spiritual traditions. It offers a sense of hope, renewal, and personal responsibility. It invites individuals to contemplate the nature of existence, the continuation of life after physical death, and the potential for spiritual growth and awakening. Whether one believes in this concept or not, it remains a fascinating topic that invites contemplation and exploration of the mysteries of life and death.

Chapter 2
Death as seen the Spirit World

Death is a natural part of life, and yet, it is often feared and misunderstood. Many cultures and religions have their own beliefs and rituals surrounding death, but what do the spirits themselves see and experience when someone passes on? According to spiritual beliefs, death is not the end, but merely a transition from one plane of existence to another.

In the Spirit World, death is seen as a beautiful and peaceful event. The Spirit is released from the physical body and enters a state of blissful freedom. There is no pain or suffering, only a sense of lightness and joy. The spirit is able to reconnect with loved ones who have passed before them, and they are greeted with open arms.

The spirits also have a different sense of time and space. While we may perceive death as a finality, in the Spirit World, time is fluid and limitless. They are able to look back on their earthly life and gain a deeper understanding of their experiences and lessons. They can see how their actions and choices have influenced not only their own lives but also the lives of those around them.

Death is also seen as a catalyst for growth and transformation. In the Spirit World, the soul is able to continue its spiritual journey with a newfound clarity and wisdom. They are able to shed the burdens and limitations of the physical world and embrace their true essence. They may choose to reincarnate and continue their learning, or they may choose to act as guides and guardians for those still on Earth.

The Spirit World also emphasises the importance of love and connection. They understand that our time on Earth is limited, and so they encourage us to cherish our relationships and live a life filled with love and compassion. They see death as a reminder to live each day to the fullest and make a positive impact on the world.

While death may be seen as a somber and fearful event in our world, the spirits in the Spirit World see it as a beautiful and transformative journey. They offer us comfort and guidance from beyond, reminding us that death is not the end, but merely a transition to another realm. By embracing these beliefs and understanding the true nature of death, we can find peace and solace in the face of loss.

Chapter 3
Reincarnation as seen by the Spirit World

Reincarnation as seen by the Spirit World is a phenomenon that has fascinated many individuals throughout the ages. It is a concept that suggests the rebirth of a soul into a new body after death, with the belief that each soul has a purpose to fulfil and lessons to learn in each lifetime.

According to those who believe in reincarnation, the Spirit World views this cycle of birth, death, and rebirth as a necessary process for soul growth and development. They believe that the Spirit World plays an active role in guiding and orchestrating the journey of each soul, ensuring that they are placed in circumstances and environments that will aid in their spiritual evolution.

The Spirit World sees reincarnation as an opportunity for souls to learn from their past mistakes, resolve karmic debts, and develop the qualities and virtues necessary for their spiritual advancement. It is seen as a chance for souls to refine their character, develop empathy and compassion, and acquire wisdom through their experiences.

From the perspective of the Spirit World, each soul is believed to have free will and is responsible for the choices they make in each lifetime. The Spirit World provides guidance and support, but the ultimate decisions and actions lie with the individual soul. This concept reinforces the belief in personal responsibility and accountability for one's actions.

The Spirit World also recognises the importance of interconnectedness and the ripple effect of our actions. They understand that every action has consequences, not only for the individual but also for those around them. Therefore, they encourage individuals to live with kindness, love, and integrity, knowing that their actions will have an impact not only in their current lifetime but also in the lives of others in future reincarnations.

Overall, the Spirit World sees reincarnation as a profound and meaningful process that allows souls to continuously learn, grow, and evolve. They recognise the interconnectedness of all souls and the importance of individual responsibility and accountability. From their perspective, each lifetime is a unique opportunity for souls to fulfil their divine purpose and contribute to the greater good of humanity and the universe.

Part 4

Communication with the Spirit World

In this section, we will explore the various methods of communication between the physical world and the Spirit World. These connections have long been a subject of fascination and intrigue, offering a glimpse into the realm beyond our own.

Mediumship is one of the most well-known ways to communicate with spirits. Mediums are individuals who have the ability to connect with and communicate messages from the Spirit World. Through their unique gifts, they act as a channel between the two realms, relaying information and providing comfort to those seeking guidance from their departed loved ones.

Seances, which have a long history dating back centuries, are gatherings where individuals come together for the purpose of communicating with Spirits. During a seance, a medium creates a conducive environment, often involving techniques such as meditation, to invite spirits to make their presence known. This collective energy and intention serve as a bridge between the physical and Spirit realms.

Channeling is another method of communication with the Spirit World. In this process, a person, known as a channeller, allows a spirit to speak or write through them. The channeller acts as a vessel for the Spirit, relaying their message with accuracy and authenticity.

These methods of communication provide a means for individuals to seek guidance, receive messages, and gain insight from the Spirit World. They offer solace and a sense of connection to our departed loved ones, as well as access to wisdom and guidance from higher realms.

Stay tuned to understand the different ways that the Spirit World can communicate with us.

Chapter 1
Mediumship

Mediumship is a fascinating and often misunderstood phenomenon that has captured the attention of people for centuries. It involves the ability of certain individuals, known as mediums, to communicate with spirits or entities from the spiritual realm. Through their heightened intuition, mediums are able to connect with the energy and consciousness of these beings and convey their messages to the living.

The concept of mediumship is rooted in the belief that consciousness continues to exist after death. According to this belief, the spirits of deceased individuals are still present in the world and can communicate with the living through a medium as a means to provide comfort, guidance, or closure. Mediumship can take various forms, such as clairvoyance (the ability to see spirits), clairaudience (the ability to hear Spirits), and clairsentience (the ability to sense the presence of spirits).

Mediums often describe their experience of communicating with spirits as a heightened state of perception. They may receive intuitive messages in the form of words, images, or feelings, which they then relay to their clients or audiences. These messages can range from personal guidance and advice to conveying important information about unresolved issues or events from the past.

Skeptics of mediumship often attribute the phenomenon to trickery or suggest that mediums are simply skilled at reading people, using cold reading techniques or educated guesses to make accurate statements. While it is true that there have been instances of fraudulent mediums, there are also numerous accounts of extraordinary experiences and validations of information that cannot be easily dismissed.

Mediumship has been a subject of interest and intrigue for researchers and scientists, and various studies have been conducted to explore its validity and mechanisms. Some researchers propose that mediumship is a result of the medium's ability to tap into the collective unconscious or the energy field that surrounds all living beings. Others suggest that it may involve telepathy or the ability to access information from the minds of living individuals.

Regardless of the explanations put forth, mediumship continues to captivate and provide solace to many individuals who are seeking answers, closure, or a connection with their departed loved ones. It offers a unique perspective on the nature of consciousness and the possibility that life transcends physical death.

In conclusion, mediumship is an intriguing and complex phenomenon that allows individuals to connect with spirits or entities from the spiritual realm. Whether one believes in its validity or not, mediumship has served as a source of comfort, guidance, and closure for many people throughout history. Its exploration and understanding can shed light on the mysteries of consciousness and the nature of existence beyond the physical realm.

Chapter 2
Seances

Seances, also known as spiritualistic meetings, have been a subject of intrigue and fascination for centuries. These gatherings, often organised by mediums or spiritualists, aim to communicate with spirits of the deceased. The word "**seance**" originates from the French word for session or sitting, and it accurately describes the atmosphere of these events - a group of individuals sitting together in a controlled environment, attempting to establish a connection with the Spirit World.

During a seance, participants gather in a dimly lit room, often adorned with candles and other mystical objects, to create an ambiance conducive to spiritual communication. The room is usually set up in a circular formation, symbolising equality and unity, with the medium or spiritualist taking a central place. The group members either join hands or place their hands upon a table to create a physical connection, allowing the flow of energy and enhancing the possibility of spirit contact. They will be requested by the medium not to move their hands so as to break the connection and cause harm to the medium sitting.

The medium acts as a channel, a bridge between the physical and spiritual realms. They claim to have a heightened sensitivity to spirit energies and are able to interpret and relay messages from the other side. The communication methods used in a seance can vary. Some mediums rely on clairvoyance, receiving visions or images from spirits, while others practicing clairaudience, hearing voices or messages from the Spirit World. The mediums may also employ tools such as spirit boards, pendulums, or automatic writing to facilitate the connection.

Skeptics often question the authenticity of seances, dismissing them as fraudulent or based on psychological manipulation. They argue that mediums use various techniques such as cold reading, where they gather information from the participants in advance and then use it to create an illusion of spirit communication. While instances of deception in the history of seances do exist, it is important to approach these events with an open mind and critical thinking.

For believers, seances provide a glimmer of hope and solace in the face of grief and loss. The opportunity to communicate with departed loved ones can bring a sense of closure and reassurance. It allows participants to seek guidance, ask questions, and gain insight from those who have passed on.

Whether one believes in the validity of seances or not, the practice continues to captivate the imagination and curiosity of many. It represents our innate desire to transcend the bounds of the physical world and explore the mysteries of the spiritual realm. Seances have left an indelible mark on our cultural history, serving as a testament to our eternal quest for answers beyond what can be perceived by the five senses alone.

Chapter 3
Channelling

Channelling is another method of communication with the Spirit World. In this process, a person, known as a channeller, allows a spirit to speak or write through them. The channeller acts as a vessel for the spirit, relaying their message with accuracy and authenticity.

Channelling refers to the practice of accessing and communicating with entities from other realms or dimensions. It is often associated with spirituality, metaphysics, and the New Age Movement. The process involves opening oneself up to receive information, guidance, and messages from these entities, which can be in the form of thoughts, visions, feelings, or words.

Channelling has been practiced for centuries in various cultures and religions. In ancient Greece, for example, it was believed that priests and priestesses could communicate with gods and goddesses through a process of channelling. Similarly, in Native American cultures, shamanic practices involve channelling spirits for healing and divination purposes.

Modern channelling, however, gained popularity in the 20th century with the emergence of the New Age Movement. It became a tool for seeking spiritual guidance, understanding one's purpose, and gaining insights into the nature of reality. Many individuals who practice channelling claim to connect with higher beings, such as angels, ascended masters, Spirit guides, or even extraterrestrial intelligences.

Channelling can take different forms and techniques. Automatic writing is a common approach, where the channeller allows a spirit or entity to guide their hand to write messages. Trance channelling involves going into a deep altered state of consciousness to allow the entity to speak through the channeller's voice. Some channellers also use tools like oracle cards, pendulums, or crystal balls to enhance their connection and receive messages.

Critics of channelling argue that it is a form of self-delusion or even a potential danger if one becomes too dependent on external entities for decision-making. Skeptics often attribute the experiences of channellers to psychological factors, such as subconscious processing or the ideomotor effect. They suggest that the messages received during channelling sessions are simply a reflection of the channeller's own thoughts and beliefs.

Nevertheless, for many practitioners, channelling provides a source of insight, inspiration, and spiritual growth. It is seen as a means to access higher wisdom and perspectives beyond the limitations of the physical realm. Through channelling, individuals seek guidance, healing, and the expansion of their consciousness.

In conclusion, channelling is a practice that involves accessing and communicating with entities from other realms or dimensions. It has a long history and has gained popularity in the modern New Age Movement. Whether one believes in the reality of channelling or sees it as a personal and psychological experience, it remains a tool for seekers of spiritual truth and self-discovery.

* * *

Part 5

The Laws and Hierarchy of the Spirit World

In this section, we will explore the laws and hierarchy that govern the Spirit World. Understanding these principles is essential to gaining a comprehensive analysis of life in the Spirit World.

Just as the physical world operates under certain laws, so too does the spirit realm. These Spiritual Laws govern the behaviour and interactions of spirits, ensuring a harmonious and balanced existence. They provide a framework for the Spirit World, guiding the actions and decisions of its inhabitants.

Additionally, the Spirit World operates on a hierarchical structure. There are different levels or planes within the spirit realm, each with its own unique characteristics and inhabitants. These planes can be likened to different dimensions, each vibrating at its own frequency and inhabited by spirits of varying levels of enlightenment and progression.

Understanding the Laws and Hierarchy of the Spirit World is crucial to navigating and comprehending the complexities of this ethereal realm.

Stay tuned to consider the Laws and Hierarchy of the Spirit World.

Chapter 1

What are the Laws that govern the Spirit World?

Just as the physical world operates under certain laws, so too does the spirit realm. These Spiritual Laws govern the behaviour and interactions of spirits, ensuring a harmonious and balanced existence. They provide a framework for the Spirit World, guiding the actions and decisions of its inhabitants.

The Spirit World is a realm that has fascinated and intrigued humans for centuries. Many cultures and religions believe in the existence of spirits or supernatural beings that exist beyond our physical world. However, the laws that govern the Spirit World are not as clear-cut as the laws that govern our physical world.

One of the most common laws that is believed to govern the Spirit World is the Law of Karma.

According to this law, every action that we take in our physical lives has consequences in the Spirit World. If we do good deeds and act with kindness and compassion, we accrue positive karma, which can lead to benefits in the Spirit World. On the other hand, if we engage in negative actions or harm others, we accrue negative karma, which can lead to punishment or negative repercussions in the Spirit World.

Another law that is often mentioned in relation to the Spirit World is the Law of Attraction. This law states that like attracts like, and that our thoughts and intentions have the power to attract certain experiences or beings from the Spirit World. For example, if we focus on positive thoughts and intentions, we are more likely to attract benevolent spirits or positive energy. Conversely, if we focus on negative thoughts or intentions, we may attract malevolent spirits or negative energy.

Additionally, some believe that the Spirit World is governed by a set of moral and ethical principles. These principles are believed to be universal and timeless, guiding the actions and behaviour of spirits. These principles may include concepts such as love, truth, justice, and compassion. Spirits are believed to be held accountable for their actions and are subjected to judgment based on how well they have adhered to these principles.

It is important to note that the laws that govern the Spirit World are not universally agreed upon and differ based on cultural and religious beliefs. Different spiritual traditions may have different interpretations of these laws and may even believe in additional laws that are specific to their own beliefs.

In conclusion, the laws that govern the Spirit World are a topic of much debate and speculation. While some believe in the universal principles of Karma and Attraction, others may have different interpretations or additional laws that govern the actions and behaviour of spirits. Ultimately, the nature of the Spirit World and its laws remain a mystery, open to individual belief and interpretation.

* * *

Chapter 2

What is the Hierarchical Structure of the Spirit World

The Spirit World operates on a hierarchical structure. There are different levels or planes within the spirit realm, each with its own unique characteristics and inhabitants. These planes can be likened to different dimensions, each vibrating at its own frequency and inhabited by spirits of varying levels of enlightenment and progression.

The hierarchy of the Spirit World is a concept that varies across different cultures and belief systems. It refers to the different levels or realms within the spiritual realm, each with its own characteristics and beings. While the specifics may differ, the underlying idea is that there are various levels of existence beyond the physical world, where souls or spirits reside.

In many indigenous cultures, the hierarchy of the Spirit World is often depicted as a vertical structure with multiple levels. At the top of this hierarchy is the supreme being or creator, who is considered the most powerful and divine. Below the supreme being, there may be different levels representing different spiritual entities, such as gods, goddesses, ancestors, and nature spirits. These levels are usually interconnected, and communication between them is possible through rituals, prayers, and spiritual practices.

In some belief systems, such as those found in certain African, Native American, or Taoist traditions, there is a belief in ancestral spirits who play a significant role in human life. These ancestors are believed to guide and protect their descendants, and their influence can be felt through dreams, visions, and signs in the natural world.

In other traditions, such as certain forms of Buddhism or Hinduism, the hierarchy of the Spirit World is structured differently. In Hinduism, for example, there is a belief in different realms or lokas, each representing a different level of existence. These realms range from lower realms of suffering and darkness to higher realms of enlightenment and liberation. Similarly, in Buddhism, there are different realms or planes of existence, including the human realm, animal realm, heavenly realm, and realms of beings in lower states of existence.

Overall, the hierarchy of the Spirit World serves as a framework for understanding the nature of the spiritual realm and the relationship between different spiritual beings. It provides a way to navigate and connect with the divine and unseen aspects of reality. While the specifics may vary, the underlying belief in a higher and deeper realm beyond the physical world is a common thread across different cultures and spiritual traditions.

Part 6

The Purpose and Lessons of Life in the Spirit World

In this section, we will explore the purpose and lessons of life in the Spirit World. As we discussed earlier, the Spirit World operates under a set of Laws and a Hierarchical Structure. It is important to understand that these aspects of the spirit realm serve a greater purpose in the development and evolution of spirits.

One of the primary purposes of life in the Spirit World is spiritual growth and enlightenment. Spirits continue to learn and evolve even after they have left the physical plane. They undergo various experiences and lessons that are designed to help them progress on their spiritual journey.

These lessons can range from personal growth to understanding the interconnectedness of all beings. Some spirits may need to learn forgiveness and empathy, while others may focus on acquiring wisdom and knowledge. Regardless of the specific lesson, the ultimate goal is to foster spiritual development and prepare the spirits for their next phase of existence.

Stay tuned to consider the purpose and lessons of life in the Spirit World.

Chapter 1
Spiritual Growth and Enlightenment

One of the primary purposes of life in the Spirit World is spiritual growth and enlightenment. Spirits continue to learn and evolve even after they have left the physical plane. They undergo various experiences and lessons that are designed to help them progress on their spiritual journey.

The ultimate goal is to foster spiritual development and prepare the spirits for their next phase of existence.

When it comes to the primary purposes of life in the Spirit World, spiritual growth and enlightenment take the forefront. In this realm, the focus is no longer on materialistic or physical aspects, but rather on the development and expansion of one's spiritual being.

Spiritual growth is the process of deepening our understanding of ourselves and our connection to the divine. It involves developing virtues such as love, compassion, humility, and forgiveness, and cultivating a sense of inner peace and harmony. Through spiritual growth, one becomes more attuned to the higher realms, gaining insights and wisdom that transcends the limitations of the physical world.

Enlightenment, on the other hand, refers to the awakening of consciousness to its true nature. It is the realisation that we are spiritual beings having a human experience, and that the essence of our being is divine. Enlightenment brings about a profound shift in perception, allowing us to see beyond the illusions of ego and separation, and experiencing the interconnectedness of all things.

In the Spirit World, souls are provided with various opportunities and experiences to facilitate spiritual growth and enlightenment. They engage in activities such as soul reflection, self-evaluation, and learning from spiritual mentors and guides. This realm offers a safe and nurturing environment for souls to explore their spirituality and discover their purpose.

The Spirit World also provides souls with the opportunity to heal and resolve any unresolved issues or traumas from their previous lives. Through the process of healing, souls are able to release negative emotions, overcome karmic patterns, and attain a state of inner peace and wholeness. This healing process is essential for spiritual growth as it allows souls to transcend their past limitations and move towards spiritual liberation.

Additionally, in the Spirit World, souls have the chance to serve and assist others in their spiritual journeys. Service is a fundamental aspect of spiritual growth, as it allows us to express love and compassion towards others and contribute to the greater good. Souls in the Spirit World engage in various forms of service, including guiding and supporting souls on earth, participating in spiritual councils, and helping to facilitate the evolution of the universe.

In conclusion, the primary purposes of life in the Spirit World revolve around spiritual growth and enlightenment. It is a realm where souls are given the opportunity to deepen their understanding of themselves and their connection to the divine, heal and resolve past traumas, and serve others in their spiritual journeys. This realm offers a higher level of consciousness and a deeper connection to the divine, allowing souls to experience the true nature of their being.

Chapter 2
Lessons to be learnt in the Spirit World

These lessons can range from personal growth to understanding the interconnectedness of all beings. Some spirits may need to learn forgiveness and empathy, while others may focus on acquiring wisdom and knowledge.

Regardless of the specific lesson, the ultimate goal is to foster spiritual development and prepare the spirits for their next phase of existence.

The Spirit World is a realm that is often mysterious and unknown to us as humans. It is a place where the souls of the departed go after death, and it is believed to hold valuable lessons and insights for those who are still living. In this chapter, we will explore some of the lessons that can be learned from the Spirit World and how they can be applied to our lives.

One of the first lessons that can be learned from the Spirit World is the importance of living a life of purpose. In the Spirit World, the souls of the departed have a chance to reflect on their lives and see the impact they had on others. They can see how their actions, both positive and negative, affected the people around them. This teaches us that our actions in this world matter and that we should strive to live a life of purpose and meaning.

Another lesson that can be learned from the Spirit World is the importance of love and compassion. In the Spirit World, souls are able to feel the emotions of others and experience the consequences of their actions. This teaches us that love and compassion are not only important for our own happiness, but for the well-being of those around us as well. It reminds us to treat others with kindness and empathy, as we never know the burdens they may be carrying.

The Spirit World also teaches us the lesson of forgiveness. In this realm, souls are able to see the impact that holding onto grudges and resentment has on their own well-being. They are able to recognise the freedom and peace that comes with forgiveness, and the negative effects that holding onto anger can have. This lesson reminds us of the importance of letting go of past hurts and moving forward in our lives.

Lastly, the Spirit World teaches us the lesson of gratitude. In this realm, souls are able to see the beauty and abundance that exists in the universe. They are able to appreciate the simple joys of life and recognise the blessings that they have. This teaches us to be grateful for the present moment and to not take our lives for granted.

In conclusion, the Spirit World holds valuable lessons for us as humans. It teaches us the importance of living a life of purpose, of showing love and compassion, of practicing forgiveness, and of cultivating gratitude. By incorporating these lessons into our lives, we can strive to live a more fulfilling and meaningful existence.

Part 7

Exploring Different Beliefs and Views About the Spirit World

In this next section, we will explore the different beliefs and views about the Spirit World. It is fascinating to see how diverse cultures and religions have their own interpretations of the Spirit realm. From ancient practices to contemporary beliefs, the concept of life after death is a topic of great interest and debate.

The Spirit World is a place of healing

One common belief is that the Spirit World is a place of healing and purification.

The importance of karma

Many religions emphasise the importance of karma and the need for spirits to balance their actions in order to progress to higher realms.

Reincarnation

Other belief systems focus on the idea of reincarnation, where spirits are believed to be reborn in new bodies to learn and grow.

Communication with spirits

The concept of communication with spirits is also prevalent in many cultures. From mediums and psychics to religious rituals and ceremonies, people seek to connect with their departed loved ones or spiritual guides for guidance and reassurance.

Stay tuned to explore different beliefs and views about the Spirit World.

Chapter 1

The Spirit World is a Place of Healing and Purification

One common belief is that the Spirit World is a Place of Healing and Purification.

The concept of the Spirit World has fascinated humans for centuries. It is believed to be a realm where the souls of the departed go to live on after death. In many cultures, the Spirit World is seen as a place of healing and purification, where individuals can find solace and seek redemption.

The idea of the Spirit World as a place of healing and purification stems from the belief that the human soul is innately flawed and requires cleansing to achieve spiritual wholeness. In this realm, souls are said to undergo a process of purification, shedding their past sins and negative energies, and emerging as enlightened beings.

One of the fundamental principles underlying the belief in the healing and purification of the Spirit World is karma. According to the Law of Karma, every action has consequences that affect the individual's future lives. It is believed that in the Spirit World, one must face the consequences of their actions and atone for their past mistakes.

For those who have lived a life filled with negativity and wrongdoing, the Spirit World offers an opportunity for redemption and growth. Souls are said to undergo various trials and tests designed to challenge them and help them learn from their past mistakes. Through this process, they are able to acquire knowledge and wisdom, ultimately leading to their Spiritual upliftment.

The Spirit World is also believed to be a place of healing, where individuals can find solace and release from the burdens of physical existence. Here, they can let go of their earthly troubles and pain and experience true peace and serenity. Souls are said to receive guidance and support from higher beings, such as Spiritual guides and mentors, who assist them in their journey towards Spiritual growth.

Additionally, the Spirit World is seen as a realm of interconnectedness, where the souls of the departed can interact and communicate with both the living and other souls. It is believed that loved ones who have passed away remain connected to us, offering their love, guidance, and protection from the Spirit World.

The belief in the healing and purification of the Spirit World provides individuals with hope and comfort, especially in times of grief and loss. It offers the assurance that death is not the end, but rather a transition to a higher plane of existence, where one can find solace, healing, and redemption.

In conclusion, the Spirit World is seen as a place of healing and purification, where souls undergo a process of atonement and growth. It provides individuals with hope and comfort, knowing that there is life beyond death and that their loved ones who have passed away are still connected to them. The belief in the healing and purification of the Spirit World offers solace, guidance, and a sense of interconnectedness, reaffirming the belief in the power of the soul's journey towards spiritual wholeness.

* * *

Chapter 2

Understanding the Importance of Karma

Many religions emphasise the importance of karma and the need for spirits to balance their actions in order to progress to higher realms.

Karma is a concept that is deeply rooted in Indian philosophy and spirituality. It is the belief that every action we take, whether good or bad, has consequences that will ultimately affect our present and future lives. This idea of cause and effect is not limited to a single lifetime but extends across multiple lifetimes, forming a cycle of cause and effect known as samsara.

Understanding the importance of karma is essential because it helps us realise that we have the power to shape our own destiny. Our actions and choices are not determined by external forces or predetermined fate but are entirely within our control. This notion empowers us to take responsibility for our actions and strive to make ethical and moral choices.

Karma teaches us that by being mindful of our thoughts, words, and deeds, we can cultivate positive karma. Positive karma leads to positive consequences, such as happiness, success, and good health, while negative karma results in negative outcomes, such as suffering, failure, and illness.

Moreover, karma emphasises the interconnectedness of all beings. Our actions not only affect ourselves but also impact others around us. Kindness and compassion towards others generate positive karma, helping to create a harmonious and supportive society. Conversely, harmful actions breed negative karma, leading to disharmony and discord.

Understanding karma also teaches us the importance of forgiveness and letting go of past wrongs. Holding onto anger, resentment, and the desire for revenge only perpetuates negative karma and keeps us trapped in a cycle of suffering. By forgiving others and ourselves, we can break free from negativity and move towards a more peaceful and fulfilling life.

Furthermore, karma encourages us to live mindfully and consciously in each present moment. Being aware of our thoughts, intentions, and actions allows us to choose wisely and avoid creating negative karma. It reminds us to pause and reflect before acting impulsively, ensuring that our actions align with our values and beliefs.

In conclusion, understanding the importance of karma is crucial for personal growth, moral development, and creating a harmonious society. It emphasises the power and responsibility we have in shaping our own lives and the world around us. By cultivating positive karma through mindful actions, compassion, and forgiveness, we can create a brighter and more peaceful future for ourselves and future generations.

Chapter 3
Reincarnation

Other belief systems focus on the idea of reincarnation, where Spirits are believed to be reborn in new bodies to learn and grow.

Reincarnation, also known as rebirth or transmigration, is a belief that is deeply rooted in many Eastern religions, including Hinduism, Buddhism, Jainism, and Sikhism. The concept of reincarnation involves the idea that after death, the soul is reborn, or transmigrates, into a new body. This cycle of birth, death, and rebirth continues until the soul achieves liberation or enlightenment, breaking free from the cycle of reincarnation.

The belief in reincarnation is based on the fundamental principle of karma, which is the Law of Cause and Effect. According to this principle, every action a person takes in their current life will have consequences in future lives. These consequences can be positive or negative, depending on whether the action was virtuous or sinful.

The belief in reincarnation provides a comprehensive explanation for the disparity among individuals in terms of their circumstances, abilities, and moral virtues. It suggests that these disparities are a result of actions performed in past lives. Those who have accumulated good karma will be born into better circumstances and possess greater abilities, while those with bad karma will face hardships and limitations.

Reincarnation also offers the opportunity for spiritual growth and self-improvement. Each new life presents a chance for the soul to learn from past mistakes, rectify them, and progress towards spiritual liberation. It is believed that through multiple lifetimes, the soul evolves and ultimately reaches a state of perfection and unity with the divine.

Moreover, the concept of reincarnation promotes a sense of accountability and responsibility for one's actions. It implies that individuals are responsible for their own fate and that they have the power to shape their future through their present actions. This belief encourages individuals to lead moral and virtuous lives, as their actions will determine their circumstances in future lives.

Although the belief in reincarnation is not universally accepted, it has had a profound impact on the cultures and societies that embrace it. It has shaped their understanding of life, death, and the purpose of human existence. It provides solace in times of difficulty and offers a sense of hope, knowing that every life is an opportunity for growth and spiritual realisation.

In conclusion, the belief in reincarnation is a foundational concept in many Eastern religions. It revolves around the idea that the soul undergoes a cycle of birth, death, and rebirth until it reaches spiritual liberation. This belief provides an explanation for the disparities among individuals and encourages moral accountability and self-improvement. Overall, it has shaped the world view and values of millions of people, offering them guidance and hope in their journey towards enlightenment.

Chapter 4

The Concept of
Communication

The concept of communication with Spirits is also prevalent in many cultures. From mediums and psychics to religious rituals and ceremonies, people seek to connect with their departed loved ones or spiritual guides for guidance and reassurance.

Communicating with spirits has been a topic of interest in various cultures throughout history. Different cultures have their own beliefs and practices when it comes to connecting with the spiritual realm. These beliefs often reflect the cultural traditions, religious beliefs, and values of the people.

In Western cultures, communication with Spirits is often associated with mediums who claim to have the ability to connect with the deceased. These mediums use various techniques such as channelling, séances, and tarot card readings to communicate with spirits. Many people in Western cultures view these practices as a way to seek guidance, closure, or comfort from loved ones who have passed away.

In contrast, indigenous cultures around the world have their own unique beliefs and practices when it comes to communicating with spirits. For example, in Native American cultures, the use of rituals, ceremonies, and sacred objects such as drums, feathers, and herbs are common in connecting with the spiritual realm. Native Americans believe that spirits are present in all living beings and natural elements, and they communicate with them through prayers and offerings.

Similarly, in African cultures, there is a strong belief in ancestral spirits. Ancestor worship is an important aspect of many African traditional religions, and people often communicate with their ancestors through rituals, dance, and music. These rituals are believed to honour and seek guidance from the spirits of their ancestors.

In Asian cultures, such as Chinese and Japanese cultures, ancestor worship and communication with spirits are also common practices. Ancestral altars are often built in homes, and offerings are made to the spirits of the deceased. In some cases, mediums or spiritual leaders are consulted to communicate with the spirits and gain insight or guidance.

In many pagan and ancient religions, such as Celtic or Norse traditions, communication with spirits is seen as a way to connect with nature and the spiritual forces that govern the universe. These cultures often involve rituals, divination, and the use of symbols and sacred sites to communicate with spirits and gain spiritual wisdom.

Overall, while the beliefs and practices surrounding communication with spirits may vary across different cultures, they all share a common thread of seeking guidance, wisdom, and connection with the spiritual realm. These cultural beliefs and traditions reflect the deep-rooted human desire to understand and connect with the mysteries of life and the afterlife.

Join us in the next section as we explore myths and misconceptions surrounding the Spirit World.

Part 8

Debunking Myths and Misconceptions Surrounding the Spirit World

In this next section, we will delve into the myths and misconceptions that surround the Spirit World. As we explore the various beliefs and views, it is important to distinguish fact from fiction and shed light on the truth.

The Spirit World is a dark and malevolent place

One common misconception is that the Spirit World is a dark and malevolent place. This perception often stems from popular culture and fictional portrayals of ghosts and hauntings.

The Spirit World is a realm of love, light and healing

However, many spiritual traditions and religious beliefs emphasise that the Spirit World is a realm of love, light, and healing.

Communicating with Spirits is dangerous or forbidden

Another myth is that communicating with spirits is dangerous or forbidden. While caution and discernment are essential in any spiritual practice, the ability to connect with the Spirit World can be a source of comfort and guidance for many individuals.

Join us in this section as we debunk these myths and misconceptions, providing a clearer understanding of the true nature of the Spirit World. By dispelling these falsehoods, we can open ourselves to a deeper exploration of this enigmatic realm.

* * *

Chapter 1
The Spirit World is a Dark and Malevolent Place

One common misconception is that the Spirit World is a dark and malevolent place. This perception often stems from popular culture and fictional portrayals of ghosts and hauntings.

The common misconception that the Spirit World is a dark and malevolent place is one that has been perpetuated throughout various cultures and belief systems. It is a misconception that stems from fear and ignorance, rather than actual knowledge or understanding of the Spirit World. In reality, the Spirit World is a realm of immense beauty, love, and enlightenment.

The notion of the Spirit World being a place of darkness and malevolence is often influenced by religious teachings and cultural superstitions. Many religions depict the afterlife as a place of judgment and punishment, where sinners are condemned to eternal suffering. This fear-based ideology has instilled a sense of dread and negativity around the Spirit World.

However, for those who have deeply studied and experienced the Spirit World, they will tell you a different story. The Spirit World is believed to be a realm of pure energy and consciousness, where souls exist in their true form. It is a dimension where love and compassion reign supreme, and where souls continue to grow and evolve.

One of the primary misconceptions about the Spirit World is that it is solely inhabited by malevolent beings such as demons or evil spirits. This idea is rooted in fear and fictional stories rather than actual spiritual understanding. In reality, the Spirit World is home to a myriad of beings, from spirit guides and angels to deceased loved ones and ascended masters. These beings are here to assist and guide us on our spiritual journey, offering wisdom, support, and love.

Furthermore, the Spirit World is a place of enlightenment and learning. Souls in the Spirit World have the opportunity to review their life experiences, gain insight into their actions, and learn valuable lessons. It is a realm where personal growth and spiritual evolution are paramount.

It is essential to challenge and question the misconceptions surrounding the Spirit World. By seeking knowledge, exploring different spiritual practices, and connecting with your intuition, you can gain a deeper understanding of the true nature of the Spirit World. It is a realm of love, light, and infinite possibilities.

In conclusion, the common misconception that the Spirit World is a dark and malevolent place is unfounded. The Spirit World is a realm of beauty, love, and enlightenment. It is important to challenge these misconceptions and gain a deeper understanding of the true nature of the Spirit World. By doing so, we can open ourselves up to the infinite possibilities and guidance that the Spirit World has to offer.

Chapter 2

The Spirit World is a Realm of Love, Light, and Healing

Many Spiritual traditions and religious beliefs emphasise that the Spirit World is a realm of love, light, and healing.

The belief in the Spirit World as a realm of love, light, and healing is embraced by various individuals and communities around the world. While this belief may differ in its specific interpretations and practices, the common thread lies in the idea that the Spirit World is a benevolent and compassionate realm that offers solace, guidance, and healing to those who seek it.

In many indigenous cultures, the belief in the Spirit World is deeply ingrained. These cultures view the Spirit World as an integral part of their daily lives, and they often engage in rituals and ceremonies to connect with and honour their ancestors and spiritual guides. The spirits are seen as benevolent beings who can provide guidance, protection, and support to the living. The emphasis is on maintaining a harmonious relationship with the spirits through prayer, meditation, and offerings.

Spiritualists and followers of New Age philosophies also embrace the belief in a loving and healing Spirit World. They believe that the Spirit World is populated by angels, spirit guides, and ascended masters who are dedicated to guiding and assisting humanity. These beings are believed to be highly enlightened and compassionate, offering love, wisdom, and healing to those in need. Spiritualists often engage in practices such as channelling, mediumship, and energy healing to connect with the Spirit World and receive messages and healing energy.

For believers in the Spirit World as a realm of love, light, and healing, the connection with this realm can provide profound comfort and reassurance. In times of grief, loss, or illness, the belief in a benevolent Spirit World can offer solace and hope. It provides a sense of continuity beyond the physical realm and a belief in the existence of a greater purpose and meaning to one's life.

Furthermore, the belief in the Spirit World as a realm of love, light, and healing can also inspire individuals to cultivate compassion, kindness, and forgiveness in their daily lives. This belief encourages the recognition of the interconnectedness of all beings and the importance of nurturing love and harmony in our relationships and interactions.

In conclusion, the belief in the Spirit World as a realm of love, light, and healing is held by various individuals and communities across different cultures and belief systems. This belief offers solace, guidance, and hope in times of need and inspires individuals to cultivate compassion and harmony in their lives. Whether it is through indigenous traditions, spiritualism, or New Age philosophies, the belief in the Spirit World can provide a profound sense of comfort, connection, and healing.

Chapter 3

Communicating with Spirits is Dangerous or Forbidden

Another myth is that communicating with spirits is dangerous or forbidden. While caution and discernment are essential in any spiritual practice, the ability to connect with the Spirit World can be a source of comfort and guidance for many individuals.

The myth that communicating with spirits is dangerous or forbidden has been a subject of debate and controversy for centuries. Many cultures and religions have held the belief that contacting spirits is a taboo practice that can lead to negative consequences. This notion has been perpetuated through various mediums such as literature, movies, and religious teachings.

However, it is important to question the validity of this myth and explore the reasons behind its existence. One possible reason for the fear surrounding spirit communication is the fear of the unknown. Humans tend to be cautious when dealing with things they do not understand, and the realm of spirits falls into this category. Our lack of knowledge and understanding about the nature of spirits and their intentions can lead to fear and mistrust.

Moreover, organised religions often discourage or forbid spirit communication due to the belief that it can lead to spiritual possession or manipulation. They argue that the spirits we encounter are not always benevolent and can have ulterior motives. In this view, communicating with spirits can open a door to the unknown and invite negative energies into our lives.

However, it is important to note that not all cultures and belief systems view spirit communication as dangerous or forbidden. In fact, many indigenous cultures have incorporated spirit communication into their spiritual practices for centuries. They believe that spirits can offer guidance, wisdom, and healing when approached with respect and proper ritualistic practices.

Furthermore, the rise of Spiritualism in the 19th century challenged the prevailing notion that spirit communication was dangerous. Spiritualists believed that communication with spirits could provide comfort, guidance, and proof of an afterlife. Although spiritualism was met with skepticism and criticism, it played a significant role in shifting the perception of spirit communication from being purely dangerous to being a potential tool for spiritual growth.

In conclusion, the myth that communicating with spirits is dangerous or forbidden is a complex issue that has been shaped by cultural, religious, and historical factors. While caution and discernment are necessary when engaging in spirit communication, it is crucial to approach this practice with an open mind and respect for the unknown. By dispelling the fear surrounding this concept, we can explore the potential benefits and insights that may arise from connecting with the spiritual realm.

Part 9

What does the Spirit World look like?

What the Spirit World looks like and what we will experience when we get there is an enigma. All we can do is to listen to people who write and talk about the same, and piece together their words just as if we were piecing together a jigsaw puzzle, one step at a time. But you must remember that we make our own Spirit World by our words and actions one day at a time...We were given personal responsibility to each find our own Nirvana. If this did not happen we would not understand the process which would lead us to our final destiny....love...light and God!

Below are quotes of people who claim they have had near-death experiences:

"Since none of us has died, death remains unfamiliar and unknown. However, a few people have visited the Spirit World through near-death experiences, dreams, and visions. We can learn much about death and the next life from their accounts."

— Dscourses of Brigham Young, compiled by John A. Widstoe, (Salt Lake City: Deseret Book 1954), pp. 368-369

"Our bodies are composed of visible tangible matter . . . What is commonly called death does not destroy the body, it only causes a separation of spirit and body, but the principle of life, inherent in the native elements, of which the body is composed, still continues"

— Brigham Young

The chapters that follow in this section will hopefully bring us solace in contemplating our passage to the Spirit World:

• We Are Not Left Alone When We Die

- The Spirit World Will Be Glorious but Familiar
- There Will Be No Strangers
- Death is Not a Thing to Fear
- Death Brings with It Hope, Light, and Love
- Mary Ann Ross (Deceased) via Leslie Flint

Chapter 1

We Are NOT Alone When We Die!

One such insight we learn from these accounts is that in the first moments after death, newly-departed spirits are often met by a guide who escorts them to the Spirit World.

It is comforting to know that loved ones or angels will greet us when we leave our mortal bodies and help us know where to go.

"In a moment I was out of the body, and fully conscious that I had made the change. At once, a heavenly messenger, or guide, was by me. I thought and acted as naturally as I had done in the body, and all my sensations seemed as complete without as with it,"

— Lrenzo Dow Young (Early 1800s)

He went on to say,

> "...the personage with me was dressed in the purest white. My guide, for so I will call him, said 'Now let us go'"

> — Lorenzo Dow Young (Early 1800s)

(Marlene Bateman Sullivan, Gaze Into Heaven; Near-death Experiences in Early Church History, (Springville, Utah: Cedar Fort, Inc., 2013), 27-30).

Tom Gibson

Tom Gibson, who had a near-death experience following a heart attack, shared that his friend Daniel came to escort him to the Spirit World. He wrote:

> "The world was different from this one. I'm not sure how I got there . . . I just followed Daniel. It seems as if all I had to do was think of where I wanted to be, and I could go there at any speed I wished. . . We continued walking for a while and I noticed someone on the path ahead of us. . . As we got closer to the individual on the path, I could see and feel that he was a magnificent person, and it was . . . I felt overwhelmed as I looked at him. He was bathed in light. Daniel asked if I

knew who that was, and I answered, yes; it was Jesus Christ.

— Tom Gibson

"When we got close to the Saviour, I felt a tremendous love emanating from him. It's hard to describe, but you could feel it all around him, and I felt a similar enormous love for him. I fell at his feet—not because I thought about it, but because I couldn't stand"

— Tom Gibson

(Marlene Bateman Sullivan, Gaze Into Heaven; Near-death Experiences in Early Church History, op cit. pp. 89-90).

* * *

Chapter 2
The Spirit World will be Glorious BUT Familiar

It is natural to be curious about what the Spirit World looks like. Some people who visited there have given clear and vivid descriptions, such as

Brother Pettersson

He said it resembled the world he knew on earth. He wrote:

"There were cities and villages, lakes and rivers, fields and gardens, houses and mansions, temples and palaces, flowers and animals of great beauty and variety. The people were busy. Some were building, some were planting, some harvesting"

— Brother Pettersson

(Marlene Bateman Sullivan, The Magnificent World of Spirits; Eyewitness Accounts of Where We Go When We Die, (Springville, Utah: Cedar Fort, Inc., 2016), 87-92)

John Powell (1867)

In 1867, John Powell wrote:

> "Daniel next led me to a city. It was a city of light—similar to cities on earth in that there were buildings and paths; but the buildings and paths appeared to be built of materials which we consider precious on earth. They looked like . . . that is they resembled marble, and gold, and silver, and other bright materials, only they were different—the buildings and streets seemed to have a sheen, or to glow. The entire scene was one of indescribable beauty. . .
>
> — John Powell (1867)

"There was another feeling that went with it. On earth there always seems to be some-thing . . . you know how things bother you here. There is always some problem trou-bling you. Either its health, or money, or people, or war, or something. That was missing there. I felt completely at peace, as if there were no problems which were of concern. It wasn't that there were no challenges—it's just that everything seemed to be under control. It was such a wonderful feeling that I never wanted to lose it"

— John Powell (1867)

(Marlene Bateman Sullivan, Gaze Into Heaven; Near-death Experiences in Early Church History, op cit. pp. 89-90).

Chapter 3

There Will Be NO Strangers

President Spencer W. Kimball taught us that familial relationships and friendships forged on earth will continue on in the next life.

President Spencer W. Kimball

He said:

> "To the unbeliever [death] is the end of all, associations terminated, relationships ended, memories soon to fade into nothingness. But to those who have knowledge and faith in the promise of the gospel of Jesus Christ, death's meaning is . . . a change of condition into a wider serener sphere of action; it means the beginning of eternal life"

President Spencer W. Kimball

(Edward Kimball, (compiled and edited), Teachings of Spencer W. Kimball, (Salt Lake City: Bookcraft, 1982), 39).

Thomas S. Thomas

Thomas S. Thomas also testified that relationships endure beyond this life. He declared:

> "The grand greeting you first receive is from your closest of kin—father, mother, brother and sisters—and all that are near and dear to you who passed from earthly life and arrived in the Great Beyond before you."

— Thomas S. Thomas

He continued,

> "I realised that I met no strangers in the meeting and greeting of the millions of souls there. . . . There were two groups of souls I met there. One group had been to earth and departed before me from there, and the other group was waiting their chance to go to earth. None of either of these were strangers to me; I had always known them"

— Thomas S. Thomas

(Marlene Bateman Sullivan, Gaze Into Heaven;
Near-death Experiences in Early Church History, op
cit., 98-102).

Chapter 4

Death is NOT a Thing to Fear

We need not fear death, for when we depart this life, we will be freed from earthly pain and filled with joy.

Brigham Young

Brigham Young said:

> "We shall turn round and look upon it [death] and think, when we have crossed it, why this is the greatest advantage of my whole existence, for I have passed from a state of sorrow, grief, mourning, woe, misery, pain, anguish and disappointment into a state of existence where I can enjoy life to the fullest extent as far as that can be done without a body"

— Brigham Young

(Brigham Young, Journal of Discourses, vol. 17, 26 volumes, (Liverpool, 1854-86), 142).

Thomas S. Thomas

Just as a mother forgets the pain of childbirth once her child is in her arms, so we will forget the pains of earth life and find comfort and joy.

> "All mental powers were restored. The fond memories of the past returned . . . your soul is endowed with wisdom and knowledge and filled with everlasting love. . . . Distance is no barrier to transmit thought without instruments, or to travel under your own power. Your vision is magnified there; your future view is plain; desire for knowledge is inexhaustible; you are master of yourself; intelligence is the key to all realms which makes an endless trail to all advancement and is a place of satisfaction and joy to the soul. . . . to the soul. . . . Time is figured on a different basis than in earthly life"

— Thomas S. Thomas

(Marlene Bateman Sullivan, Gaze Into Heaven; Near-death Experiences in Early Church History, op cit., 98-102).

* * *

Chapter 5

Death brings with It Hope, Light, and Love

Perhaps the most important thing we learn from those who have visited the Spirit World is that Heavenly Father and His Son, Jesus Christ, are divine Beings who love and watch over us and that we can live with them again if we follow the example of our Saviour, Jesus Christ, and obey God's commandments.

These experiences also teach us that our moments on earth are just that—moments—and that eternity stretches before us. Reading these accounts instills upon our minds the importance of making more productive use of our time on earth. We can reevaluate our priorities to direct our time and energy growing and mastering ourselves. Everyone has sins to repent of, faults to change into strengths, and frailties to overcome.

"For behold, this life is the time for men to prepare to meet God; yea, behold the day of this life is the day for men to perform their labours. . . . if we do not improve our time while in this life, then cometh the night of darkness wherein there can be no labour performed"

— (Alma 34:32-33)

These accounts comfort our souls with the knowledge that in the next life, we can live in a sphere governed by love and light—a place of great beauty and everlasting peace.

Admonition of Nephi

To achieve this blessed state, we would do well to follow the admonition of *Nephi*:

"Wherefore, ye must press forward with a steadfastness in Christ, having a perfect brightness of hope, and a love of God and of all men. Wherefore, if ye press forward, feasting upon the word of Christ and endure to the end, behold, thus saith the Father: Ye shall have eternal life"

— (2 Nephi, 31:20)

Chapter 6

Mary Ann Ross (Deceased) via Leslie Flint

Flint, Leslie (medium) Recording: Mary Ann Ross

On 20th January 1969

Leslie Flint was a very powerful physical medium whose lifetime spanned from 1911 to 1994. His mediumship was unique because he connected to spirits via a voice box, which appeared above his head.

On 20th January 1969, a lady named Mary Ann Ross came through Leslie. This is now regarded as one of the best and most charming descriptions of life in the Spirit World. Charming because she gets reacquainted with her long lost love.

Mary Ann Ross describes the way she died, her departure from Earth and her awakening in the

Spirit World. She explains how everything was strange to her at first, as she meets the friends and family who she thought were dead and gone.Then Mary describes meeting her long-lost love after many years and how, together, they attend a spiritual musical concert like nothing she had ever experienced before...

This message is one of many that comes from Leslie's archives, which are now maintained by The Leslie Flint Trust (1997-2022).

MARY ROSS ON LIFE IN THE Spirit World

Mary's first experience of entering the Spirit World

"But it's very odd. It was as if the whole room was full o' light. And I could see all sorts o' people around. There was my mother and my father and my brother, who'd died many years before. And Nellie. She was a friend. One o' ma few friends, that had died only a few weeks...they were all in the room and I thought I was having a dream, about my people. But it was Nellie, who came and she put her arms around me, and she kissed me on the face. And it was warm and real. And my mother came, she kissed me too. And they took my hands, and the next thing I know it was as if I was floating through the window and then everything went black. I cannot remember a thing until I woke up. And I was in a bed in a very nice room, with rafters and beams and things - like an old house. But it was cosy and friendly and the sun, that I thought, was shining through the window. And there was my mother, but she did not look the same as when I saw her in ma dream, as I thought. She looked young, as I'd seen her in the picture that used to hang in my bedroom, when she was married, many years before. And she'd got a white dress and she had a black bow ribbon in her hair - so like I'd seen her in early pictures, when I was very young. We used to have everything - collection of old photos, that mother'd keep in the tin. Yes, it was just as if I was seeing her as she was then. She said to me that I was alright and that I'd nothing to worry about and I was not going back, and I thought this is just a dream. And then she said no, it's not a dream, it's real...you're alive now, you're not to worry about anything. And she said, soon, when you're really recovered over this, she said, we'll go out we'll meet all sorts of people that you used to know when you were a wee bairn, you know, when you were young."

Mary not realising that she was dead

"I could not quite see and understand, I could not realise at that stage that I was dead. It was like a beautiful dream. Then there was a dog jumped on ma bed and this really gave me a fright, in a way.

116

Not that I was afraid of dogs, I was fond of animals, but this was a dog that we'd had many years ago, that ma father adored and that was killed by a cart, many years ago, when I was, oh - in my twenties, I suppose. And this dog we called it Nipper. And do you know, to see Nipper jump on this bed startled me and I just couldn't realise. My mother said, of course we've animals here too. Ah, I thought well this is - you know, I just couldn't understand it, if they were dead. As my mother said, that there'd be animals too. And she said, oh that's nothing. She said, out in the yard, she said, you'll see a lot of other animals too."

Mary is surprised at seeing animals

"I just couldn't take to this at all, I couldn't believe. You know, when you've been brought up as I was, to a religious way of life, you know, you didn't automatically begin to think of animals being here. And then again, I thought this was too natural to be heaven. I thought it would be quite different and that it would all be, well, like one sees in pictures and religious books, you know the angels and wings an the - - - you know. This didn't seem right, I thought it must be a dream or that I'd wake up, but no. I don't know how long I must ha' been in this way, but I know that I felt different."

Mary's request to see herself in a mirror

"I felt as if I was light as air and I was curious about myself and I said I'd like to see myself in the mirror and my mother laughed at me and she said we don't have mirrors here. Mirrors are not necessary, you can see yourself when you know yourself. You don't have to look into a mirror to see how you look or how you are. I didn't understand this at all, but all I know, that I felt so different. I felt so young and ma body seemed light. I just felt as if I could get up and dance around the room. But my mother said no, not for the moment, you just wait a wee while, you see."

Mary becoming aware how she could quickly transport herself just by power of thought

"And the next thing I must have dozed off, at least that's what I thought I did. But it wasn't really quite dozing off. Next thing I know was that I was walking down, what appeared to be, a lane, you know. It was beautiful, with trees either side and beautiful fields and I could see cattle. And there were all sorts of animals that I'd seen in picture books. And once years ago, my mother when she was well, many years before, and my father was alive, we'd gone to Edinburgh and I remember we went to a place where there were animals. And, it was very interesting to see all the different animals there. I just couldn't understand, you know, there were beautiful creatures and they were wandering around and no one felt afraid, I didn't feel afraid."

Mary describing birds and music

"Ah, I don't know and there were birds in the trees and they were whistling and singing and there was music. And I can only say it sounded like music to me, but there was no - nothing that I remembered in music. But I was very musical myself, though I never had any opportunity to study music, but I always liked music. And I could hear music and sounds, which were - oh it was a strange thing as if there were the sounds of nature. And there was also the animals and the birds and it was all so wonderful, as if it all blended together. And I remember walking and walking on this road and somehow, I had no feeling of tiredness and I came to the end of, what I suppose was the lane and there was a beautiful white house. Beautiful house, all white and yet, it wasn't painted white."

Mary being reignited with a lost love

"And the first thing that struck me was that, although I could see the house was beautifully kept, but it wasn't paint. It had a sort of lustre about it, like mother of pearl. And yet it was chiefly white and yet there were soft shades of other pastel colours. It was as if it was all aglow and as I came to this house, a man came out of the door and my heart gave a jump, that's if I had a heart, but I just felt as if - oh I couldn't believe this. But it was a young man that I was very fond of, who I'd turned down, but it wasn't because I didn't love him. It was because I realised that I couldn't have married him because it meant that I had to give up my parents who were getting old and in need of care and attention. And I didn't feel that it was right to put a burden upon a man, of someone else's parents, no matter how fond he was of me and I turned him down. He ever got married and he moved away from the district soon afterwards and I lost touch with him for many years. Then he came out of this house and he looked just as he'd looked, oh, many years before in his thirties, tall and dark and, in those days though he had a moustache. And the thing that, I suppose it's silly how things strike one, but he had not got a moustache an' all, but I could recognise him quite well in spite of that. But he came rushing down the front of his garden path and met me. And he put his arms around me and, oh he made such a fuss of me and I felt so overwhelmed, you know. And I felt, oh, as if for the first time, that I was wanted. I suppose in a way I shouldn't say that, because I was very much wanted by my parents and I was very fond of my parents, and they were very good parents to me, but I don't know, but, it is a different feeling I can't explain that, and he said ah, at last you've come to me and he says, this time you'll no turn me down. And I did not know what to say to him and then, all of a sudden it seemed as if, in the garden, all the flowers began to blossom."

Rossiter tells Mary that the flowers represented the love between them

"Ah, I don't know how to explain this without sounding silly, but all the flowers suddenly seemed to grow and, it was as if the garden came alive. And there were all kinds of flowers there, flowers that I remember from the Earth and flowers I'd never seen before. And there was one clump of huge, tall orange flowers, like poppies, but they seemed to go on and on and on. And I thought, if they don't stop growing they're going to be taller than the house. I thought, how stupid this is, I'm so happy here, with Rossi - Rossiter, you know - and yet all the time, in spite of all my happiness and meeting him and feeling at ease and feeling happy, I could see this growth of poppies, as I called them, growing taller and taller until they became like huge trees. And then all of a sudden, the petals began to open and they began to, like, droop."

"When I say that, I don't mean to say that they were dying, it's as if they opened up and the petals folded down and made like, a kind of umbrella. And there were all these beautiful orange flowers, like umbrellas. And we went and we stood, at least I think we stood, underneath them. It was as if, through the petals of these enormous orange flowers was a beautiful light, and it seemed to have warmth and seemed to have a glow. And he was smiling about this because I said, I've never seen such big flowers and I've never seen such beautiful colours and I've never seen flowers so tall."

"And he said, ah, he said until you came, although I planted many seeds in my thoughts, that one day I'd have a beautiful garden. It wasn't until you came, it was then that I knew, that I'd have a garden which I could be proud of. And he said, these poppies, as you call them, is my love, that has been growing all the years I've been watching over you. And he says, they're symbolic of us in a way and, he said, our love together. And now we can be free. He said, come into the house."

Mary describing a house that she had always wished for

"So, and again, I can't say if I walked or if I floated, but it was as if my feet never touched the ground. And I remember going into the house and it was just as I'd always wished and dreamed. It was not a big house but it was, it was bigger than anything I'd been used to and everything seemed to be perfect, just as I would always wanted to have had myself, and the furniture, everything. And it was solid and real and there were such pretty colours and such a wonderful feeling of home. And he said, now, he said, we're together and now he says we can make up for lost time. I had never felt so happy and then I thought about my Mamma and my Father and he said that's alright, he said you've finished. Now you have your own life, to be shared with me. But we will keep in touch and we can go and see them whenever we wish and they can come and see us too."

Mary talking about a home she had always wished for, and a piano. Rossiter tells Mary that she can have all she desires here....

"He says you have so much to learn. And all of a sudden, in the corner of the room, as he was saying this, something I had not seen before. I saw a piano. I don't know why I never saw this at first, but, because I'd always wanted to be a musician. I'd always wanted to be able to play. I'd always loved music very much indeed. And he had been a music teacher and I did not realise, I suppose it should have struck me, that he would naturally still be interested in music and that he would, if possible, have a piano and he said, now, he says, you can have one of your heart's desires, you can become musical and I would teach you and you can learn. And, ah, I was so happy and so thrilled. It was just as if my youth had come back to me and all the opportunities that I desired and all the things that mattered most to me, were mine. Ah, I know this sounds so crazy."

Rossiter helping Mary to play the piano

"Then he sat at the piano and he played like an angel, all the beautiful music that I used to love so much. And the short time that I knew him, he used to play in the Kirk [Church] and he used to play sometimes in the meetings that used to be held in the Social, in the village, you know. And he was playing all the things that I'd loved so much, you know. And not only those things, but other things too and it was as if, through him, I was almost, you might say, mesmerised into being able to play myself. Because I don't remember in a sense, having lessons. Of course I must have had lessons, but it was as if when I sat down later at the piano, and he stood beside me, that is, my fingers sort of, automatically went to the right notes."

"And I know now that it was him, working through me in a strange way, mentally helping me and helping my fumbling fingers, you know. And, ah, I know this sounds so extraordinary, then he said we go, sometimes to what you would call concerts and you hear the great people which makes me, he said, feel so insignificant, but it gives me hope that I might eventually one day be able to play beautifully. And I was not cross with him, but I thought well how stupid. And I said, but you play beautifully, you have a wonderful touch, you know. And he said, no, no, no, you haven't heard what I have heard and I said, well I'm quite happy with you and the way you play. He said, well you must come with me and we'll go to concerts."

Mary visiting a concert for first time

"And eventually he took me to one place in particular, which was in a, I suppose you'd call it a town, because there were all sorts of houses and large buildings where people were living and there was a huge place, with many steps and when I first looked at all those steps I thought, my, my, what a lot of steps. You'd get so tired climbing up all those steps and the funny thing was that I did not feel tired at all. I did not even feel as if I'd climbed steps. But nevertheless, we went into this great place and it was so vast. It must have held thousands of people. And there on a platform was a beautiful piano, the most beautiful thing I'd seen in my life."

"It was enormous, much bigger than any other piano I'd ever seen or heard of. And I should imagine it had three tiers of keys it was a tremendous thing and very, very beautiful. And it's as if it was made of mother of pearl, it had the most beautiful colours and tints. And then a beautiful creature [a man] came on, he was tall and nice looking and his hair was long and he had fine features and he sat down and he started to play."

"Well, I'd never heard anything like it. It, the funny thing is, that it seemed as if there were three of the keyboards being used at the same time and yet there was only the one pair of hands. And when or how, I don't know how the other keyboards were played. I did not see his hands go to the top two keyboards, only the lower. But I could see the depression of notes on the other keyboards and I can only assume that in some way they were all connected up together, I maybe wrong, but it was extraordinary. The sound, it was as if you were carried away by it and as if you were enveloped by it, and as if you lost sense of place and time and everything. And as if you were, in a kind of way, with the music and part of the music and you lost sight the hall and the people and even the pianist after a time."

"It was as if you were transported in a most strange way, as if you were part of the music and as if it was talking to you and helping you to understand. It was an extraordinary experience, then of course I knew what my friend had said and meant, when he said the difference in his playing. It was, of course a great experience for me, but as I said to my friend, I quite appreciate, and it was a wonderful experience, but I still like the way you play just as much. And I realise as I said that, I meant it."

Extraordinary things happen here...

"At the same time, looking back, I know that it was a bond between us, but I realise that this other experience was something beyond ordinary music. And I, now of course, know that all sorts of extraordinary things do happen here, and that there are many aspects, I think you say, of experience, which one couldn't begin to explain."

"But I'm very happy now, but I must say that I've had some fantastic experiences which I would like to recount from time to time, if it's permitted you know. Because I think it might be interesting to other people."

Mary talking about the experience of dying. If you know about death you know what to expect

"And as far as people dying, no one need worry about it at all. It's the most wonderful experience. And of course at first, it's a shock, but you soon get over that, and if you know about it beforehand, you know what to expect, which is a great help. I didn't you see and a lot of people don't and they don't realise that they're dead at first. Takes them a little while to understand, you see?"

Mary was asked what she was doing know apart from her music

"I am teaching children in a wee school and I'm very happy with that. I always loved children and I always would have like to have had children myself, and now I teach. But I will come and talk to you if I may, sometime again."

END OF RECORDING

Embracing the Mystery
of the Spirit World

In conclusion, as we wrap up our comprehensive analysis of life in the Spirit World, it is important to acknowledge that while we have explored various beliefs and debunked myths, the Spirit World remains a mysterious and elusive realm. It is a realm that surpasses our human understanding and invites us to embrace the unknown.

Through our journey, we have learned that the Spirit World is not a dark and malevolent place as portrayed in popular culture. Instead, it is a realm characterised by love, light, and healing. We have also discovered that communicating with spirits, while requiring caution and discernment, can provide comfort and guidance.

By dispelling myths and misconceptions, we have gained a clearer understanding of the Spirit World's true nature. However, there is still much to be explored and discovered. It is through embracing the mystery that we can continue to unlock the secrets of this enigmatic realm and deepen our connection to the spiritual realm.

Join us in future publications as we further unravel the mysteries of understanding spiritual matters one step at a time.

Together, let us continue to explore and expand our knowledge of this fascinating and infinite realm...

Bibliography

Flint, Leslie (medium): Recordings
https://www.leslieflint.com/mary-ann-ross/mary-ann-ross
Kimball, Edward (compiled and edited), Teachings of Spencer W. Kimball, (Salt Lake City: Bookcraft, 1982), 39)
Sullivan, M. B (2018)
https://www.ldsliving.com/5-insights-into-the-Spirit-world-from-those-who-have-seen-it/s/82344
Sullivan, M. B: Gaze Into Heaven; Near-death Experiences in Early Church History, (Springville, Utah: Cedar Fort, Inc., 2013), 27-30.
Sullivan, M.B: Gaze Into Heaven; Near-death Experiences in Early Church History, op cit. pp. 89-90.
Sullivan, M. B: The Magnificent World of Spirits; Eyewitness Accounts of Where We Go When We Die, Springville, Utah: Cedar Fort, Inc., 2016), 87-92
Sullivan, M.B: Gaze Into Heaven; Near-death Experiences in Early Church History, op cit., 98-102)
Sullivan, M.B: Gaze Into Heaven; Near-death Experiences in Early Church History, op cit., 98-10
Young, Brigham: Journal of Discourses, vol. 17, 26 volumes, (Liverpool, 1854-86), 142)
Young, Brigham: Dscourses of Brigham Young, compiled by John A. Widstoe, (Salt Lake City: Deseret Book 1954), pp. 368-369

Acknowledgments

If it wasn't for my parents and my grandparents, I would not have been able to finally live the life that I was always meant to live.

God bless you. Wendy x

About the Author

One of the most valuable sources of insight into the afterlife comes directly from spirit themselves. Through various forms of communication, spirits seek to guide us on our journey and alleviate any fears we may have about death and the absence of an afterlife. This new perspective gives rise to a fresh way of thinking - A New Age. It is this trans-formative mindset that my books strive to cultivate.

I sincerely hope that after reading this book you will approach the concept of life after death with an open mind. By doing so, you can unlock a deeper understanding of how to navigate both this world and the next with purpose and fulfilment. My books are dedicated to promoting this transformative perspective.

If you wish to read further accounts provided by spirits of what it is like in the Spirit World, I would suggest that you listen to the many tape recordings of Leslie Flint (link provided in Bibliography).

Wendy

Printed in Great Britain
by Amazon

39686442R00086